1,001 Bits of Wit

Thomas Wilson

PAGE PUBLISHING, INC.
New York, NY

Second originally published by Page Publishing, Inc. 2018

ISBN 978-1-64298-604-4 (Paperback)
ISBN 978-1-64298-605-1 (Hardcover)
ISBN 978-1-64298-603-7 (Digital)

Printed in the United States of America

If I were you,
who would you be?

Freedom ain't free
but truth is.

When others do your
thinking, you get the
blame and they
get the credit.

There is an ocean of sweat
between flabs and abs.

The bits of wit that are in this book are original, humorous, challenging, and true. It took more than three decades for me to write them. Wanda Martin challenged me to put them in print. I accepted her challenge.

T. H. Wilson Sr.
PO Box 367
Lufkin, TX 75902-0367

Follow Thomas Wilson Sr. on Facebook
And call 936.676.7~~065~~.

7026

Contents

To the Reader

I HOPE YOU WILL enjoy this compilations of maxims and quotes I have formulated over the last thirty-seven years. It would be worthwhile to date, initial, and record wise spur-of-the-moment statements you often make. They can be humorous, serious, outlandish, and timely. Write them down. They belong to you. You can share them with us in a few years.

A few of the thoughts in this book have obvious Biblical implications. The rest are personal. A friend from Houston, Wanda Martin, encouraged me to publish these quotes. She is a most serious Bible student, and I practiced some quotes conversing with her. Now, do your own. Enjoy.

T. H. Wilson Sr.
March 2008

Special Thanks

I THANK MY LORD Jesus Christ first and foremost. I am indebted to the few members of the North Lufkin Church of Christ. They are the audience of encouragement that sit at my feet on the Lord's Day to receive God's gospel. It would be futile to attempt naming those of you that encourage me to continue writing. We need each other. Life is a challenge. If it were otherwise, how boring our existence would be.

Man is a striving creature. I have striven to share these quotes hoping they will bring a ray of hope. If they evoke one chuckle, the writing will not have been in vain. Please continue to pray for me. It is good to use your talent lest you should hide it under a bushel basket.

Bro. T. H. Wilson Sr.

Wilson's book

GRACE JUAREZ/The Lufkin Daily News

Local author T.H. Wilson poses for a photo with his new book "1,001 Bits of Wit" that recently released from Page Publishing Company. The book can be purchased on Amazon, Barnes & Noble, Google Play and iTunes.

936-676-7026

Words of Encouragement

THE LORD SHOULD BE glorified in our lives individually and collectively. Some of us are self-motivated; others need an external force to jumpstart us and away we go. I am self-motivated. There are people all around us achieving things great and small. You could be the next Olympic champion or Nobel Prize winner. Take inventory of what you have to offer humanity. The world needs every good and perfect gift that God sends to be developed.

It does not take much effort to plan great things. It does demand discipline for the plans to become actuality. I pray that you will let your gift be made known soon. You can do it so get to it. This is your time to shine. If not now, when? Set your sails today, and the winds of achievement will welcome you. Now, what?

Bro. T. H. Wilson Sr.

Chapter 1

General Maxims

1. Keep shaking the tree; the fruit will fall.
2. For the good to workout, the bad must be outworked.
3. Regret is not having achieved what was possible.
4. Memories bridge the gap between then and now.
5. The unexplored is yet unclaimed.
6. He who dares is no stranger to danger.
7. To not give is to not live.
8. Seek not comfort in a deadly habit.
9. The road of fantasy leads to the land of what if.
10. Change will not ask your permission.
11. Wishing without working is dumb.
12. Love never grows old.
13. Thoughts fill the air waiting for you to grasp them.
14. The world of self is without smiles.
15. Stand tall if you will stand.
16. How sweet the prayer none can repeat.
17. A friend chastises without hesitation.
18. The best laugh is the one you evoke.
19. Love without trust is like a guitar without strings.
20. Innocence stares down false accusers.
21. Tyrants are never prepared to die.
22. Worry is ever looking, never seeing.
23. Pain is the firstborn of preparation.

24. The first to be deceived is the deceiver.
25. Money loved is an idol god.
26. Life is a series of diminishing steps.
27. Persistence is the face that never looks away.
28. The prepared demands opportunity.
29. Losers are masters of excuses.
30. When all seems lost, the champion prevails.
31. A covetous heart is never satisfied.
32. He that can count the molecules in the air understands women.
33. When a rich man loves money, his poverty returns.
34. Prejudice is a sly chameleon full of venom.
35. A life without balance is like two hands on one wrist.
36. Every routine can be improved.
37. You do not have to explain why you are fat.
38. I prefer giving to lending.
39. Many athletes train to inflict pain for gain.
40. Where there is no laughter, there is no youth.
41. The less you work, the older you get.
42. Hate hath no halo.
43. When you doubt, you are out.
44. The undisciplined child will soon have a cellmate.
45. Kindness even moves the mindless.
46. Have you stopped worshipping yourself?
47. Free throws in life are not guaranteed.
48. The inanimate rocks know Jesus Christ is Lord.
49. Win in overtime, if you must.
50. Obesity takes no prisoners.
51. When you compromise your convictions, then what?
52. Losing your temper can cost your freedom.
53. Life will demand your best at some point.
54. I must be about me before I can be about you.
55. God did not make women to rule over men.
56. The break room is often the date room.
57. Cheap office hanky-panky can get real stanky.
58. A franchise player must never flinch.
59. Interviews are not for losers.

60. Who complains about being underworked and overpaid?
61. Interesting people are ageless.
62. Experience minus commonsense spells disaster.
63. Modern women often demand equal opportunity badness.
64. With all things equal, the smartest player wins.
65. You do not have to act stupid to get attention.
66. A friend loves to bail you out.
67. Your stock and trade should be stocked and never traded.
68. Religious experience can be delusional.
69. Compete with a controlled fury and radical aggressiveness.
70. All of the criminals are not in Washington.
71. Sometimes you have to travel in uncharted path.
72. A smoker's clothes should never touch a baby's nose.
73. Jesus Christ drank wine in moderation.
74. The Devil is not lazy.
75. He who leans at the tape often wins.
76. Talent without drive is like a car without fuel.
77. What is commonsense to me is nonsense to another.
78. Better the hard but hopeful than easy but hopeless.
79. An unforgiver has no hope.
80. He who sleeps in class is a candidate to sleep under the bridge.
81. When your date is as talkative as a tombstone, it is time to move around.
82. Smokers will blow smoke anywhere we let them.
83. What good is a day without a dragon to slay?
84. Jesus Christ will judge atheists also.
85. When you do it, you know it is done.
86. If you do not envision the gold, get out of the race.
87. Some never think for themselves
88. Laziness lives next door to craziness.
89. You must rise from the rubble when the roof caves in.
90. Poverty is a perpetual curse.
91. Things are really bad when you boil the bullet then eat it on wheat bread.
92. Never be intimidated.
93. Be smart or be silent.

94. Energy makes it happen.
95. Burying your clock at the North Pole will not freeze time.
96. You never run the same race twice.
97. Our children think, the chain of command is a rapper's bling-bling.
98. Hard times might be closer than your next check.
99. You will be wrong sometimes.

Chapter 2

After-Dinner Thoughts

100. Do good today without ulterior motives.
101. Know the difference between involvement and commitment.
102. Turn roadblocks into starting blocks.
103. Leave a spot on your back for someone else to pat.
104. Motivation separates the best from the rest.
105. Deal or get dealt.
106. A harsh word can start a war.
107. Bad habits take their toll in due time.
108. Neither friends nor foes respect cowards.
109. All the commotion is about the spot at the top.
110. Make every move a picture; every word immortal.
111. When you turn sideways and look in the mirror, what do you see?
112. Thoroughbreds do not run long races.
113. History is marred when bad leaders start real wars under false pretenses.
114. The unwise will tempt the inescapable snare.
115. Ever wonder if your secret is known?
116. Never count yourself out.
117. Make every smile fit for a poster.
118. What would life be like without rain?
119. The octopus of sin has invisible tentacles.
120. The greatest fan of the arrogant is himself.

121. Love makes you laugh for no other reason.
122. Giving makes life worth living.
123. Better to choose health than wealth.
124. Life is not a drill.
125. Snakes do not have ears, but they know you are coming.
126. A lazy man will not taste sweat.
127. Good wisdom rejected becomes a curse.
128. Love welcomes reassurance.
129. Is your appetite on cruise control?
130. A fault admitted screams for correction.
131. The forest is deep so find your own tree.
132. Who will you blame the next time?
133. God is really the goal.
134. Many demons might leave if we stopped wrestling with them.
135. You never regret doing your best.
136. I love you is so simple yet so hard.
137. Sometimes a woman wants to hear what she wants to hear.
138. Life gets more interesting when you pay attention.
139. A good laugh is contagious.
140. Relax and max is the name of the game.
141. Great men rise again.
142. Everyone loves a fat baby and a fat paycheck.
143. A wise man is the target of fools.
144. How long before the presidency is outsourced?
145. Are we now the land of the duped?
146. The louder the music, the surer the hearing aids.
147. Do aliens abduct fat people?
148. Mercy cushions the day of reaping.
149. You cannot walk like brass and ask for diamonds.
150. One mistake can a bad future make.
151. Makeup artists cannot cover a lie.
152. Decatur, Georgia, gave us Gwen Torrence and good bass fishing.
153. Both thieves went to the Cross alive yet dead; one was taken down dead yet alive.
154. Many stone mountains are not in Georgia.

155. God did not make women for women.
156. Drugs are never free.
157. What is the primary difference between love and lust?
158. Intemperance leads to the maze of excess.
159. Men on the down low are really lowdown.
160. Longways or lengthwise, God made woman for man.
161. Beware of the Up Women, Down Men pervert.
162. Relativism is the enemy of Christianity.
163. What would be the verdict if we judged ourselves?
164. A mother smiles when her baby burps.
165. Energy determines age.
166. Kindness makes a mean man exhale.
167. A pharmacist is a licensed drug dealer.
168. There is a difference between touching and grabbing.
169. A true warrior defies all odds.
170. A song in the heart puts a sparkle in the eye.
171. Some men are bald by choice.
172. Night falls when daylight sleeps.
173. The bed of incest is never soft.
174. The son of a lonely woman is a jealous kid.
175. A meek woman conquers the toughest of men.
176. It is a shame to play without your "A" game.
177. A dog is a dog's best friend; a woman, a man's.
178. Looking younger requires work
179. A spy has no friends.
180. If you cannot dance, clap your hands and bobble your head.
181. Dehydration precedes health cessation.
182. We are all experts when we get it right.
183. There is often one move between underdog and top dog.
184. Are there any Walmart stores in Vermont?
185. The daughter of a possessive father is a crisis-in-motion.
186. The ego muscle requires daily massaging.
187. What happened when the woman took over in Eden?
188. It is better to think for yourself.
189. Character is neither bought nor sold.
190. Beware of the mouth of sarcasm.

191. A wimp's twin is a boneless chicken.
192. Your enemy knows when you begin to click.
193. Dark clouds do not always bring rain.
194. He that is predictable is expendable.
195. There is a spy in every neighborhood.
196. Heaven is silent when a woman cries.
197. A bad law is easier passed than repealed.
198. Righteous judgment is not a reproach.
199. The difference between good business and robbery is jail time.

Chapter 3

Family Encouragement

200. Sound judgment is not a by-product of experience.
201. The champion has a thirst to be first.
202. The hero is but a step from skid row.
203. A forgiving spirit has reason to smile.
204. Spontaneous vitality turns heads.
205. The envious heart has no peace.
206. When the wise genie got out, he broke the bottle.
207. Speculation is a matter of opinion.
208. Convicts often get religion before their parole hearing.
209. A slave to carnality is an eternal fatality.
210. Memories connect all portions of time.
211. There is no wise way to waste time.
212. A gang on the northside is a club on the southside.
213. Patience is the key that fits all locks.
214. The slower you go, the longer it takes.
215. Every action is attached to a memory.
216. Adversity flees in the face of hope.
217. Contrary winds blow hot-sand and gold dust.
218. Fear dilutes strength.
219. A coward is a flunky for every mean person.
220. The trash man has his day.
221. Right can seem so wrong.
222. Granting a child's wish is magical.

223. Overtime should be an equal opportunity period.
224. Judicial tyranny threatens the fabric of democracy.
225. Every flower has a secret to share.
226. The stare of a brave man makes an army flee.
227. The strong should be just as gentle.
228. He who listens is never lonely.
229. Love is the perfect passion.
230. Never spill everything you feel.
231. A good cook never has to boast.
232. A baby's smile has melting power.
233. That is straight up and downtown.
234. Boredom will surely knock.
235. Balance is easier with both feet on the ground.
236. The sun shines brighter when a woman laughs.
237. Negligence leads to indigence.
238. The world is turning, and the cameras are rolling.
239. No hours in, no dollars out.
240. The winds of regret visit us all.
241. One man's joke is another man's insult.
242. A coward prefers humbling to rumbling.
243. The nightmare begins when the dream ends.
244. Bad leaders force the masses to rebel.
245. Your friends also have faults.
246. Jesus Christ cannot fail.
247. Stripes do not a sergeant make.
248. Hungry is the hobo with an ego.
249. A godly man should live godly.
250. A banker is a treasure hunter.
251. The scars of war last a long time.
252. Tears of combat never cease to fall.
253. War changes a man.
254. Racism is the enemy of brotherhood.
255. Many underestimate the devil's power.
256. A man should act like a man.
257. The word of God is the true absolute.
258. To trust God is most comforting.

259. A pleasant surprise is always welcome.
260. Walking forth out of the ashes removes all doubt.
261. God is too awesome to be denied; too holy to be lightly spoken of.
262. The fool has no fear of God yet.
263. Gluttony is a deadly addiction.
264. God's word exposes the scholar's madness, and the layman's hypocrisy.
265. The heart of love has its pain palpitations.
266. The path of truth is so obvious; only few find it.
267. The remedy for a foolish breakup is an instant makeup.
268. Beware of the woman with the potato pie and the teary eye.
269. Public safety should trump a company's voluntary compliance.
270. The all-you-can-eat buffet is the red carpet to obesity.
271. The masses prefer a perverted gospel.
272. God alone is holy and reverend.
273. False friends will set you up to take you down.
274. Thank, God; it is what He permits it to be.
275. A one-sided romance is like a half-done biscuit.
276. When you blow it, you know it.
277. The Devil is more powerful than all of man's weapons.
278. Walk with pride even when you are broke.
279. A dilemma is a predicament on the front burner.
280. A clapping crowd soon becomes a murderous mob.
281. A rifle without bullets is a fighting man's death sentence.
282. Nosy people act concerned.
283. Outlandish women resent strong men.
284. Extreme pacifism is most illogical.
285. Kids that cutup should be butchers.
286. When you owe a friend, only two people know it.
287. Entreaty is preferred to scolding.
288. What flatters one will shatter another.
289. A good day is to wake up.
290. Some invade what others evade.
291. Observe your surroundings before you get surrounded.
292. Easy money has strange bedfellows.

293. A thinking cap is useless on an empty head.
294. The choice is between classy and classless.
295. The charred lungs of a smoker will make him breathless.
296. A bum never stops bumming.
297. Those that start wars should be on the front lines.
298. A policeman that rescues you is never a pig.
299. A guilty conscience is the surest witness.

Chapter 4

Friend to Friend

300. A mean woman has no mate.
301. Every woman needs her own roof.
302. A graceful woman is unforgettable.
303. He that is timid soon becomes a coward.
304. A soft spoken bully is still a bully.
305. The working poor outshines the poor not working.
306. To be defenseless is senseless.
307. Sabotage is in the hands of the builder.
308. A visit to the smile shop is free.
309. Some befriend only to betray.
310. A selfish son covets his father's crown.
311. A father also has feelings.
312. Evil lurks in every human heart.
313. A sweet kiss has lasting embers.
314. Perception is the precursor to reality.
315. A lover's embrace is full of fire.
316. When the feeling is gone, you will know.
317. One chance might be all you get.
318. Pretend that you do not know it all.
319. Abused health is full of vengeance.
320. Corporations only play hardball.
321. Never sheepishly shrug off an insult.
322. A fat person always has something to lose.

323. No one rushes to answer an unwanted call.
324. He that skates on thin ice will go down.
325. If you cannot swim, do not make waves.
326. Finding fault requires no skills.
327. A preacher has no privacy.
328. Intense desire trumps degree of difficulty.
329. Your enemies hate when you straighten up.
330. The rich will always trample the poor.
331. Rich men will sell the flag for a buck.
332. Walking with your eyes closed gets attention.
333. Death has no pity.
334. Every life has its fiery furnace.
335. A wise man knows when not to stop.
336. Robots are not to be loved.
337. Airplanes built by enemies have a mind of their own.
338. Friends help you do better.
339. Performance has first chair.
340. A triple-reverse might work, and it might not.
341. He that is predictable is not interesting.
342. Death equalizes the playing field of life.
343. Good words keep an empty seat warm.
344. When a crooked judge dies, his gavel becomes a boomerang.
345. Some wait until you recover, then call.
346. A smart driver pulls over when sleepy; a wise driver pulls over before.
347. Hang tough, or tough will hang you.
348. Finishing second just turns me off.
349. Life would be much better if all politicians lived off minimum wage.
350. He that is without a dream has no purpose.
351. A deceitful woman can date two brothers.
352. Do not stay out of touch too long.
353. A smoker's family might die first.
354. Speeders pay more to arrive later.
355. Them that got are never at peace.
356. God has a database of judicial misconduct.

357. Angels peer when a man holds a woman's hand.
358. Play smash-mouth, or stay in the house.
359. To beat the odds, you must defy them.
360. There is a scamp in every camp.
361. Your undisciplined child has a date with a prison warden.
362. Some neighbors are doing just what you think they are doing.
363. Your secret is soon public knowledge.
364. She was pretty, but she was fat.
365. Great peril awaits those sincerely misinformed.
366. Every day is somebody's last day.
367. Live as if you die today; you might.
368. Angels appear when you have a flat without a spare or jack.
369. A good wife helps a midget become a giant.
370. Deep water is not for non-swimmers.
371. A chemical coma is good when it is medically induced.
372. If you cannot fake it, how can you make it?
373. Evil thoughts bombard every heart.
374. A fool thinks he can always try again.
375. Remember, the big fish still eats the little fish.
376. A smoker will cough eighty-one times for every puff.
377. One day in battle is all some will see.
378. Dehydration is the origin of much illness.
379. A rich man's joy is a poor man's shame.
380. A possessive son will not let a widow remarry.
381. To be predictable is to be expendable most of the time.
382. It is better to be a wife, then a mother.
383. When people shack; one is shameless, and one is willing.
384. When lawmakers flinch, sedition is born.
385. A troublemaker is seen afar off.
386. The fruit of the Holy Spirit does not grow on limbs.
387. Talent without tenacity is like love without affection.
388. If you were me, who would I be?
389. The hogs will always find the slop.
390. The adversary will poison your pill.
391. Nature exhales when a baby is born.
392. Defining moments do not have to be isolated events.

393. The gold is for the bold.
394. A kind word lifts heavy burdens.
395. Every day is somebody's birthday.
396. If you have not played the fool, you will.
397. A kiss without passion is like an ice cube under the eyelid.
398. A man's special lady should always feel special.
399. Chitterlings are not fit for human consumption.

Chapter 5

Patriotic and Religious

400. He that loves money has green ink for blood.
401. Criminals will always have weapons.
402. Poverty with its frills teaches a man survival skills.
403. Many humans would go to jail if animals could kiss and tell.
404. A baby born out of wedlock is no less a baby.
405. A love triangle is a hazardous entanglement.
406. A house is no shabbier than its occupant.
407. You should salute the flag you live under.
408. There is no compromise between truth and error.
409. A man in debt will soon walk alone.
410. Integrity is not a lottery prize.
411. Love has everything to do with it.
412. God will get the last laugh.
413. Cursed is the man that strikes a woman or child.
414. Neither angels nor eunuchs marry.
415. A brief fling can be a deadly thing.
416. Every child has legend potential.
417. You can sit in the river and die of thirst.
418. The Devil wants you to just smoke one more cigarette.
419. There is no second place in war.
420. Man takes the steroids, then they take the man.
421. A wounded king never forgives.
422. Never expect a lion to be a vegetarian.

423. Pretty women have the advantage.
424. He that buries his talent, buries himself.
425. Every gift is not an act of love.
426. Some friends overdose on a need to know your business pill.
427. An unfaithful woman will never trust a man.
428. When all else fails, a woman cries.
429. A lie is impotent in eternity.
430. Every leader is a rebel.
431. Life gives no man a blank check.
432. To rise again, you must conquer what took your strength away.
433. A warrior hastens to the ultimate challenge.
434. A man's destiny will not let him sleep long.
435. Even Heaven had one bad day.
436. You will never grab what you do not reach for.
437. The most plentiful meat in Washington is baloney.
438. Children take the weakest parent captive.
439. The short answer might be better.
440. He who trembles before contrary winds is soon blown away.
441. Fight not at your enemy's convenience.
442. There is no love without pain.
443. Truth has no relevance in a prejudiced heart.
444. The ice house has no mercy.
445. Never try to walk on water in a cement suit.
446. You do not have to be asleep to dream.
447. Courtesy does not necessarily imply complicity.
448. A friend respects your space.
449. The sincerest compliments are spontaneous.
450. Enemies delay what they cannot derail.
451. If you must stand alone for right, stand alone.
452. The Devil sees nothing wrong with shacking.
453. Speech patterns quickly change on death beds.
454. Acute drug intoxication has turned Hollywood into Follywood.
455. Every man thanks God for woman.
456. Self-perpetuating theatrics has driven godly reverence from pulpits.
457. Too much wine will not let you leave in time.

458. Christ made wine for men to drink with temperance.
459. Death never accepts bribes.
460. Dreams are free but pay big dividends.
461. Second-hand smoke is no joke.
462. Pecan pie is as unhealthy as it is delicious.
463. A healthy family is a wealthy family.
464. Many experienced men legalized slavery.
465. Unflossed teeth want out.
466. You do not need a pond to take a bath.
467. Some stage a setback to make a comeback.
468. It is not what you drive, but what drives you.
469. A politician's speech has a peculiar odor.
470. Protesting on Pennsylvania Avenue will get quick results.
471. Companies cooking the books consider pension funds as assets.
472. Someone will believe whatever is said.
473. I have never seen a cancerous lung on a billboard.
474. Most listen when it is too late to matter.
475. Superstars have little time for sound doctrine.
476. An effeminate man has no problem with wearing female clothing.
477. Never bring cigarettes to church.
478. When Eve stepped out, sin stepped in.
479. Man has a problem with moderation.
480. Congressmen should outsource tobacco and keep the jobs.
481. Politicians regret having only two sides of a mouth.
482. God blessed women with long hair.
483. Obese educators took physical education out of schools.
484. Your negligence is your enemy's friend.
485. All trash is not in the dumpsters.
486. It probably is what you hope it ain't.
487. Make your enemies wish you were pretending.
488. Remember any well you poison.
489. Kindness is an oasis of hope in a desert of depression.
490. Combat is something you never forget.
491. Words carry weight that cannot be measured.
492. Convict conversions rarely last beyond the prison gates.

493. Lonely nights last longer.
494. No wound can compare to a broken heart.
495. The most unwise decision makes sense at the time.
496. Bull riders have a lot of bucks.
497. Some women are too mean to be sweet.
498. Illegal drugs are bullets without gun barrels.
499. Tyrants pretend to protect what they work to destroy.

Chapter 6

Thoughts to Ponder

500. God's camera has night vision.
501. That which never died cannot be resurrected.
502. A gang leader's gut must match his strut.
503. Intemperance has turned our fatness into madness.
504. Disease will soon accommodate the careless.
505. Abstinence is ordained of God and disdained by men.
506. The richest criminals walk free with glee.
507. Effort is the master of difficulty.
508. Difference in days should not negate love.
509. It takes eight seconds for a cowboy to be born.
510. It pays to walk with a tough friend.
511. A pregnant woman should push but not be pushed.
512. When some move in, some move out.
513. A good marriage is godly protection.
514. When you marry for money, you have the right to worry.
515. The Devil prefers counterfeit churches to money.
516. Children should never be abandoned; no parents scorned.
517. The unforgiving heart is a trip ticket to hell.
518. A made-up mind is hard to find.
519. To be decisive is to be divisive.
520. Neglect invites defect.
521. Never buy eye-drops from your enemy.
522. When lawmakers balk, protesters walk.

523. A weak body will soon die.
524. Family reunions should not require bulletproof vests.
525. Conversions do not demand convulsions.
526. Stroke your arteries lest they stroke you.
527. That which is most bizarre, pleads foul.
528. A decent woman should not dress like a Sumo wrestler.
529. Pretenders imitate contenders.
530. The tongue of envy never gives credit.
531. Men highly esteem what God condemns.
532. A fence speaks for itself.
533. Some fight, some spar.
534. The first to call need not talk long.
535. The clock of God is never reset.
536. God's girls are never manly.
537. The Devil has plenty of children.
538. Tyrants are only for a season.
539. A friend will warn a friend.
540. Man is a finite creature with infinite aspirations.
541. Let the singers sing.
542. A fool hates his rebukers.
543. The vilest racist is attracted to beauty.
544. God integrates, Satan segregates.
545. The kindest child is the best.
546. Infidelity is twin to calamity.
547. The Devil's wine is sweet and full of poison.
548. We should love our enemies, not trust them.
549. There is no comfort in obesity.
550. Health is an issue of connective tissue.
551. Home invaders come with guns.
552. Nieces and nephews are like nuts in chocolate.
553. The most unprepared will argue.
554. A loud woman is not of God.
555. The benefits of love outweigh its risks.
556. Watch the what, and the when and the why will be obvious.
557. Obesity is not an accident.
558. He that arrives on earth will surely depart.

559. Integrity is twin to intestinal fortitude.
560. When we ignore injury pain lasts longer.
561. What would politics be without scandal?
562. The hypocrite hopes you are not paying attention.
563. He that is wrapped up in himself is a small package.
564. Somebody's children will be somebody's parents.
565. Long prayers clear many throats.
566. God's time is all that really matters.
567. Some will not rest unless they are tempted.
568. Always protect your own.
569. When we give proudly, we live proudly.
570. A grave digger also has a hole.
571. A pretty smile is a master key.
572. The humble spirit rides on God's elevator.
573. Stupid retaliation forfeits championships.
574. May history speak favorably of your last night.
575. Out of the mix comes the max.
576. While hoarding wealth, he was forfeiting health.
577. Sexy is about one inch from trampy.
578. The Noble Prize needs more candidates.
579. A gluttonous man has chosen his poison.
580. Better to right the wrong than bring it.
581. A misprint must be corrected.
582. A lie cannot be recalled.
583. Never ditch your dignity.
584. Facts are quite stubborn and rightfully so.
585. Best reigns until bested.
586. Bad nutrition avoids the dietitian.
587. A fat man's scales are never right.
588. Train hard enough to defeat tough opponents and overcomes bad calls.
589. The true orator writes his own speeches.
590. A grand slam can clear some things.
591. To never say no is no way to go.
592. Get involved or get dissolved.
593. No chains can prevent love.

594. The impulsive can get repulsive.
595. Bookies cry when favorites fall.
596. An immoral act is not a civil right.
597. When schools sent prayer out, mass murders came in.
598. A diplomatic flunky is a curse to his nation.
599. When you erode inside, you corrode outside.

Chapter 7

Health and Inspiration

600. Some women are too sweet to be mean.
601. Late fees cost more to those that have less.
602. The Super Bowl creates a super hole in church attendance.
603. Woe to the man that mixes his money with God's.
604. Racists walk in the hall of Christendom with venom spewing.
605. Some mistrials are miscarriages of justice.
606. A diamond and flower for the woman of the hour.
607. Veterans give so much and receive so little.
608. Your secret lust has shelf space in the emporium of human frailty.
609. Let the majority remember, the minority cometh.
610. If a lion will be king, let him roar.
611. When vigilance sleeps, the vigilante creeps.
612. The promiscuous are also bold.
613. Wasted time cannot be retrieved.
614. Every rainbow is a promise kept.
615. Good does no good when you wait too long.
616. Peace is not in the contents of the purse.
617. You abuse the drug, then the drug abuses you.
618. There is an angel for every baby.
619. Every teardrop is a word unspoken.
620. Nobody regrets not talking too much.
621. To hit a home run, you must swing the bat.

622. Customers are not always right.
623. Love is the sweetest mystery.
624. God's reservoir is always full of compassion.
625. The Church of Christ has no pope.
626. It is easier to amend than to change.
627. A ladder has rungs for a reason.
628. God knows it before you think it.
629. Some phone calls are conveniently missed.
630. Innumerable hours of worry have not one problem solved.
631. Losers still sell blood and buy drugs.
632. Let the leader lead.
633. He who fights bullies wins friends.
634. Speak to some, talk to others.
635. The gentle hand is hypnotic.
636. A lazy man has no joy.
637. Kind words soften stony hearts.
638. The Devil trembles at the wrath of God.
639. Trauma closely follows drama.
640. God's blessings have no strings attached.
641. There is no estimated time of arrival with death.
642. Unhappy is the man with a short rope at a deep well.
643. Poverty aggravates all that it touches.
644. Chest pains get more attention.
645. File your lies for future reference.
646. Change is good for all men.
647. When Jesus Christ is with you, hell cannot prevail.
648. A reasonable woman expects men to see it her way.
649. Committees usually appoint another committee.
650. A lazy man is always between jobs.
651. The man always between jobs will get mashed.
652. A woman walks beside her man, but a good woman walks with her man.
653. Nothing goes right for fear of what might go wrong.
654. A wimp has no loyalty.
655. The Devil is not a weakling.
656. Misuse a true friend, and he still wishes you well.

657. Experts took physical education out of school, and childhood obesity runs rampant.
658. The air is polluted, and the water is drugged.
659. We never die tomorrow.
660. The Devil is the father of perversion.
661. Always be kind to the receptionist.
662. Your self-esteem is purely personal.
663. If you really want to mess it up, hire an expert.
664. Good-bye is always difficult.
665. Guilt never lets trust sleep.
666. The Devil doesn't mind sitting on the back row.
667. What secrets do animals keep?
668. A pretty smile is an unprejudiced treasure.
669. A broken heart is a bitter pleasure.
670. The elderly must be honored.
671. Refuse some invitations without apology or explanation.
672. Say only what might be recorded because it might be.
673. No one lives without a fantasy.
674. A cutting remark goes deep.
675. There are no snapshots of Jesus Christ.
676. Eve did not guide her house.
677. A man of rage is subject to a jail or hell.
678. True age is measured in energy which is worth repeating.
679. Man's hour-glass of time is finite.
680. A smoker's child is puzzled.
681. A smoker's spouse is an endangered species.
682. Women love checks that do not bounce like babies.
683. A frown is fit for a clown only.
684. Less than your best should not leave the house.
685. A delicate man has lost his way.
686. We all have moments of emotional slippage.
687. Few desire the full parameters of truth.
688. A woman is God's gift to man.
689. Wishing without working is like sleeping while walking.
690. A man is never as smart as he thinks he is.
691. A loving parent has no bad child.

692. Some never call until they fall.
693. There is no lie your adversary will not tell.
694. A scorned woman never forgives.
695. Mother's sins make you cry, but daddy's sins never die.
696. No moment is so sweet as when the right lips meet.
697. A strong man falls many times.
698. A good banker is an angel of comfort.
699. Thrash trash before thrash trashes you.

Chapter 8

Despair and Depression

700. The hand of a man that strikes a woman is cursed of God.
701. The tongue of a gentle woman is sweeter than honey.
702. Some are smarter than we think; others not as smart as they think.
703. The mercy of God neutralizes His justice according to His pleasure.
704. A clean woman keeps a clean house.
705. Without imagination, there is no nation to imagine.
706. The blood of Christ can clean-up our mess-up.
707. A leader must be able to focus in the dark.
708. There is a path through every storm.
709. To reject reality is to chase a mirage.
710. Waste your time, not mine.
711. Things get better when you win.
712. You will rise no higher than you act.
713. Boring is the relationship void of variety.
714. The bread of mediocrity will soon grow stale.
715. A debtor has no peace.
716. Dogs lick without discretion.
717. A superb performance never hurts.
718. Marathons are not run at sprint speed.
719. Are blueberries really purple?
720. Freezers sell better in Texas than Alaska.

721. If only dust mites could be exchanged for dollars.
722. The next sentence might be your last.
723. Knowing what a yoctosecond is does not make you smart.
724. A chapel is never far in Las Vegas.
725. Wherever you go somebody is there.
726. Know what you mean, and mean what you say.
727. It is most difficult to connect with now.
728. Everything after yourself is extra.
729. A man without an objective soon ceases to be.
730. Underdogs have fewer heart attacks.
731. Every living creature is dying.
732. Every bluff will be called.
733. Count your money before you sleep.
734. You can just be yourself with the Lord.
735. A doubting prayer never rises above your nose.
736. Man exists in the space between alpha and omega.
737. There is no time without change.
738. To plan and not act is beating the air.
739. Be careful how you treat your foes.
740. A lazy man sleeps more than a gorilla.
741. A wife is a most delicate creature.
742. Lawmakers are the worst lawbreakers.
743. Every man wants a son.
744. Would you rather play squash or eat it?
745. Never walk behind a hummingbird, they fly backward.
746. Men want God outside the boundaries of His word.
747. Do not rest too long.
748. The Lord never drops you off; He never forsakes His.
749. Never look like a coward unless you are one.
750. Many women prefer sisterhood to godliness.
751. Relaxation enhances concentration.
752. Self-pity is the first step to becoming a zombie.
753. The diligent answers before duty calls.
754. Knowledge plus enthusiasm equals achievement.
755. A life without variety invites anxiety.
756. A golfer without a putter is like a ship without a rudder.

757. Motivation is the victor's mojo.
758. Goals help us reach higher.
759. Faith neutralizes your foes.
760. All prayers are not accepted by God.
761. He that exercises self-control will rule many cities.
762. The courageous will conquer the strong.
763. Adversity is the warrior's bread.
764. There is security in purity.
765. Without choices, life would flow in one direction.
766. The man that bums a ride will soon be late for work.
767. When opponents are evenly matched, motivation determines victory.
768. Endurance is the ability to welcome pain.
769. Commitment is bold-face resolve.
770. A man that walks into the shadows with his head down is a failure.
771. Beauty is the impression that never grows old.
772. Midnight blindness is the mist engulfing the world of self.
773. Worry is the willing transfer of life sustaining energy to a faceless entity.
774. Sweat gives hope to the brow.
775. A dull encounter chokes the spirit.
776. Sorrow is the image of a painful reflection.
777. Poised is he that salutes the firing squad.
778. A ghost has more honor than a traitor.
779. A lucky man is most observant.
780. A moment of hesitation can cost a fortune.
781. The vigilant will shine in a crisis.
782. A genius detects the hero in every villain.
783. Good teachers are never far away.
784. The best cook has clout in the kingdom.
785. A woman that cannot cook should learn.
786. A confident man is never conquered.
787. He that perseveres will catch a white-tailed rabbit.
788. The man that acts will sign the thinker's checks.
789. Enemies can be so inspiring.

790. He that is not tempted is deceased.
791. Life is a complication of simple things neglected.
792. Money will make your children call home.
793. Shock is when two fishing buddies unknowingly lose their boat returning from the lake.
794. Sleep is a realm where fairy tales and reality mingle.
795. A good handshake is remembered.
796. A surprise to one is expectation to another.
797. Where there is life, there is sickness.
798. A friend will always love you.
799. Courtesy will feather any nest.

Chapter 9

Athletes and Workplace

800. Where there is no passion, there is nothing.
801. Sex has little to do with bodies.
802. Sometimes it's best to blow the ashes and move on.
803. The future is an extension of now.
804. Thin ice can feel so firm.
805. The greatest danger is to ignore it.
806. A pessimist has no hope in humanity.
807. Yesterday was the tomorrow of the day before.
808. Anybody can wear a uniform.
809. A strong family will weather the storm.
810. There is a prostitute in every woman.
811. A diary is a reminder of what might have been.
812. A prosecutor's greatest fear is being prosecuted.
813. Women condemn in men what they do with men.
814. The devoted turn neither left nor right.
815. A good wife is a gift from God.
816. A couple in love is easy to spot.
817. The optimist shines from the depths of despair.
818. Visualization is faith's little brother.
819. A man without interests is uninteresting.
820. Flee from a woman with uncombed hair.
821. To know how a woman thinks, ask a woman.
822. A gun bought from an enemy will jam.

823. Success is failure turned inside out.
824. The face of a sleeping infant freezes time.
825. Some women have too much testosterone.
826. When you reach the top, plant a tree and a flag.
827. The dude of shrewd is often lewd.
828. Unwelcomed opinions often come from unqualified persons.
829. There is not always evidence of what a person is.
830. During war, the land screams for rest.
831. A rebellious student goes from dormitory to reformatory.
832. He that is jealous, imitates God.
833. A man is prisoner to his darkest weakness.
834. Bad days beset us all.
835. A snail's pace is better than standing still.
836. Why do women wear micro-minis?
837. Without profit, there would be no war.
838. An exhibitionist will not close her curtains.
839. Only God is to be feared.
840. What you read in the newspaper could be a misprint.
841. A hero is one scandal from a zero.
842. Morbid obesity is not of God.
843. The dirt committed in the office never stays in the office.
844. A short-temper can get a long sentence.
845. Would you rather lose your little finger or your big toe?
846. When you doubt yourself, you have nothing left.
847. Some things we love more than we care to admit.
848. Life is a war we all must wage.
849. The Pentagon has five sides.
850. That which separates you from God is your idol.
851. When the tree has fallen, it is too late to move.
852. Tell me something you do not know.
853. Old flames are easily rekindled.
854. The difference between wanting and doing is it.
855. The procrastinator hopes to defer to the second life.
856. There comes a time when you just have to leap and hope.
857. When you connect the dots, you get the picture.
858. Controversy gets attention.

859. Some lawmen are lawless.
860. Do you blame the dam for being so weak, or the water for being so strong?
861. Autopilot will not work in life.
862. Never fret when opinions prove faulty.
863. A man with big hands should give more.
864. The true measure of man is not in feet and inches.
865. Long hair is shame to men but glory to women.
866. Knowledge defuses mysteries and unlocks enigmas.
867. He that manages time will eventually manage money.
868. Check the air in your spare before you get stranded somewhere.
869. He that will do great things must be willing to suffer great things.
870. A wise man knows there is a time to fight and a time for flight.
871. When a person shows up at the wrong time, let them know.
872. A man becomes a slave when his freedom does not matter.
873. When a problem appears, the solution beckons.
874. Man's vengeance is a detriment to love.
875. Nothing lifts a burden like a good word and a green dollar.
876. An angry man should touch neither woman nor child.
877. Helping hands are always welcome.
878. You do not have to search for friends when prosperity hits.
879. He that trusts no one will not take medicine.
880. A good deed will always come back.
881. A veteran is the first to die and the last to cry.
882. Death never fires a warning shot.
883. God will connect you so His word can protect you.
884. Satan is not to be taken lightly.
885. The Devil pretends to be God.
886. God draws every hungry soul to His Son Jesus Christ.
887. Satan will slander what he cannot destroy.
888. There is no righteousness without persecution.
889. The eyes of false friends are green with envy.
890. A friend bears gifts.
891. Love has room for one more.
892. Pure religion is scorned by the masses.

893. The mother of Jesus Christ also sinned.
894. Only Jesus Christ lived a sinless life.
895. The oft-neglected parents cry out to God.
896. The skin of a child should never be bruised or whelped.
897. Who does a good deed unnoticed by God?
898. Every thought stands naked before God.
899. False teachers are masters of speaking smooth things.

Chapter 10

Self-Examination

900. Any church will not do.
901. The Holy Spirit revealed the Holy Bible.
902. Fear will keep you poor.
903. The masses will sadly prefer tradition to truth.
904. Bullies do not like resistance.
905. Arrogance is selfish defiance of any law.
906. The glory seeker soon insults God.
907. The public is careless with its health.
908. Legal drugs are frequently dispensed in illegal quantities.
909. Some men are so weak; their tailbones have replaced their backbones.
910. Racism could not thrive without church participation.
911. Jealousy is often cloaked in sarcasm.
912. Man rejects truth and supports lies to preserve family ties.
913. The self-righteous feel little need for prayer.
914. The drug abuser will die for a high.
915. Illicit affairs start off charming but end up harming.
916. A submissive wife is applauded in heaven and scorned on earth.
917. When man steals God's money, He puts a curse on his purse.
918. Man began eating himself to death in the garden of Eden.
919. A perverted gospel can also be convincing.
920. The Devil is a master duplicator.
921. Admit your error, and you will feel better.

922. An alternative dishonoring God must be rejected.
923. The gospel of Christ is not amenable to innovation.
924. Some sidekicks should be kicked aside.
925. Doctors often lose empathy when insurance is revoked.
926. A contrite spirit can soften the heart of a hanging judge.
927. Some eyewitnesses are paid to become lie witnesses.
928. To define a check in the mail as child support is simply barbaric.
929. Positive reminiscing is therapeutic.
930. When you lose your job, you cannot tick with the clique.
931. The age of perversion defines natural as relative.
932. A fake can only ad-lib so long.
933. Even a brother might desire your energy.
934. Debauchery is a death knell even for a nation.
935. A lie only has one foot.
936. The illiterate should not be scolded.
937. The albatross of racism is alive and well in America.
938. The time to quit smoking is today.
939. A recession does not wait for the government to declare it.
940. The weather man is not wrong all the time.
941. Rich men import drugs, and poor sell them.
942. The more you sit; the fatter you get.
943. Obesity is our greatest liability.
944. One deadly habit is enough to kill you.
945. Do not confuse friendship with domination.
946. While you are complaining, remember those that cannot speak.
947. A patient man never speaks too soon.
948. How often do you pray for your enemies' prosperity?
949. What color is Santa Claus?
950. Why leave the gym and head to the donut shop?
951. If you do not want the game-winning shot, get off the floor.
952. The wealthiest man still wants more.
953. Is anyone in your house over-medicated?
954. Within a few years, we should be a surgically-reconstructed society.
955. All my teammates have an obsession with winning.

956. If you will not be productive, be gone.
957. When a winner competes, he cannot count beyond the number one.
958. Without history, life would be a most puzzling mystery.
959. Never teach your assistant all you know.
960. The blood of Jesus Christ removes all guilt from failed marriages.
961. God's woman guides the house and refrains from worldly entanglements.
962. Some women prefer to be alone with strange men.
963. When others are crawling on their knees, walk on their backs until you get to the front.
964. Foolish words are haunting boomerangs.
965. If you crash but do not burn, you will be just fine.
966. Look for something to compliment people for.
967. He that is wishy-washy will end up like the dinosaurs.
968. Sometimes a smart kid has to walk home alone.
969. Honesty shocks people in a very positive way.
970. When you put on a front, no one will get to know the real you.
971. It is better to shatter with the truth than flatter with a lie.
972. A rocking chair never travels far.
973. God is always in control, period.
974. There are no reruns in real life.
975. A genius is a strange friend.
976. Pornography is a stepping-stone to abject debauchery.
977. Life without purpose is mere existence.
978. God will not be second chair.
979. The Light of Christ dispels any darkness a human repents of.
980. Love is gentler than a summer breeze blowing across an infant's forehead.
981. When two people love each other, they have no desire to be with anyone else.
982. The person standing on the foundation of godly conviction cannot sink.
983. Jesus Christ will also judge atheists.
984. There is a whoremonger in every man.

985. Brutality in human nature is no respecter of gender.
986. The self-image of an abused woman is tenuous at best.
987. Tough men do not fight women.
988. The ashes are not used to rebuild the burned house.
989. Women cheat for a variety of reasons.
990. Men cheat for a variety of reasons.
991. Children do not hold grudges.
992. Nightfall is uniquely mysterious.
993. He that is uncouth does not cover his cough.
994. A man could hide from many things if he had no conscience.
995. Every flower has its fragrance.
996. When time is no more, the gates of eternity will swing open.
997. Those that hunger for power are never filled.
998. A bed without a loving couple is just a bunk.
999. Faith turns the wheel of God's chariot.
1000. The joy of the Lord will quell the grief of any man.
1001. God has a man to stand in every gap.

About the Author

T. H. Wɪʟsᴏɴ Sʀ. lives in Lufkin, Texas. He was born and reared in Marshall, Texas. He was married to Ruth Ann Wilson for twenty years. He is the father of seven children. He and Ruth reared four that are living in the Dallas, and Melissa, Texas area. T. H. played football and ran track at H. B. Pemberton High School in Marshall, Texas. He *still* keeps in contact with classmates of the 1966 class. No one remembers T. H. as being a shy guy. However, he takes pride in repeating the words of his best old school friend Harvey Davis Sr. Harvey lives in Houston, Texas, and although he is a renowned song leader, Harvey has said some people might think that he is a man of few words. T. H. follows suit for sarcastic humor. T. H. thoroughly enjoyed rising up as football captain and trash talking during high school pep rallies that often had Panther supporters from the city of Marshall to attend. He won bronze medals in his junior and senior years in spelling and plain writing in state competition. The UIL State Competition took place at Prairie View College back in the day. He also ran on the Elite 4×400M relay teams in state competition both years. He was the only kid to compete academically in the morning and athletically in the afternoon. T. H. has written eleven books and one religious tract. He likes to play chess and Scrabble and engage in lively discussions in subjects ranging from the Bible to politics.

In fact, he predicted in the *Lufkin Daily News* in Lufkin, Texas, on November 3, that Donald Trump would shock the world and defeat Hillary Rodham Clinton on November 8, 2016 for president. Many people laughingly felt that T. H. was having a senior moment. Their laughter was short-lived for sure. Trump won, and his Democratic and Republican friends are *still* scratching their heads. T.

H. spent years of great challenge and excitement in the US Marines. He did his time in Vietnam. He spent his entire time in the United States after Vietnam. He was at Marines Aviation Detachment in Corpus Christi, Texas, and Base Materiel Battalion Camp Pendleton, California. His MOST enjoyable moment in the Marines was when he won the hand-to-hand Close Combat Championship. He was with Fox Company Second Battalion Seventh Marines Regiment First Marine Division. T. H. comes across as laidback and easy going. However, he was demoted and missed noncommissioned officer promotion due to physically assaulting several Marines. He was honorably discharged in 1970. He gave up fishing and hunting after God blessed him to return from Vietnam.

He has been preaching the Gospel of Christ in the Church of Christ since December 22, 1971. He is a lover of life and enjoys challenging conversations. He has another book of quotes that he will submit to Page Publishing in God's time. He is thankful to Wanda Martin for challenging him to have his quotes published. Friends like James and Brenda may played an integral part in T. H.'s life as did his Sister Helen King and his oldest brother, James Artis Wilson Sr. Church friends in Lufkin include the late Elder Tom Crater and Elder Ralph Fair. He is always thankful to Sister Donya Walker and Camilla Gibbs Woods and the Gibbs Dynasty of the late Dr. S. T. W. Gibbs Jr. of the Greater Stop 6 Church of Christ in Fort Worth, Texas. T. H. obeyed the Gospel of Christ on October 10, 1971, at the Westside Church of Christ in Marshall, Texas. He preached his first Gospel Sermon under the Tutelage of the Eminent Dr. W. F. Washington Sr. of the New Golden Heights Church of Christ in Fort Lauderdale, Florida. Many others too numerous to mention are listed in heaven and earth as helpers of this ministry.

No person has the unique status of rescuing T. H. and his ministry from homelessness and despair when *all* others failed but Sister Mozell Marie Darden. He is forever indebted to her. T. H. loves to write and challenges friends and strangers to develop your talents to the utmost, and soon you can be receiving a writer's submission kit from Page Publishing Company in Staten Island, New York. I send *all* of you much love and many prayers and desire the prayers of the righteous daily.

CPSIA information can be obtained
at www.ICGtesting.com
Printed in the USA
FSHW012052140519
58145FS